FEMALE AND CATHOLIC

A Journal of Mind and Heart

FEMALE & CATHOLIC

A Journal of Mind and Heart

MARIE McINTYRE

TWENTY-THIRD PUBLICATIONS
Mystic, Connecticut

Twenty-Third Publications
P.O. Box 180
Mystic, CT 06360
(203) 536-2611

Library of Congress Catalog Card Number 86-50658
ISBN 0-89622-307-8

Cover design and illustration by Kathy Michalove
Edited and designed by Helen Coleman

Reflections that speak
For all women some of the time
And for some women all of the time

Foreword

In the twenty-odd years since the end of the second Vatican Council, one of the most important developments in American Catholicism has been the surfacing of women who have challenged some of the church's age-old assumptions about language, spirituality, and power.

Marie McIntyre's journal reveals a personal attempt by one thoughtful woman to make sense of her faith today in the light of this new debate as well as her own experience. Since this struggle parallels that of so many Catholics in these difficult decades, it speaks not only to women but to all of us.

Though she is searingly honest about how the church's rigid actions and attitudes often nullify and distort the "good news for us" that lives in the Bible and the words of Jesus, the message in these short reflections is upbeat. Catholic faith is helpful for human development, she insists. And you will hear this message of hope throughout her "journal of mind and heart."

Her essay "Discomfort" accurately summarizes the "in-between" times in which so many Catholics live today, groping through moral dilemmas with contradictory guidelines. But this situation is ideal for learning, the journal demonstrates. "Quiet Times" can deepen our personal sense of self; hearing the messages of Jesus and the prophets can strengthen our ability to make choices we believe in and can live by.

One of the great strengths of this journal is the author's ability to relate such messages to her own life. It speaks of long experience in doing so. When she writes about "Fear" or "Suffering," she shows how the former blocks and the latter aids our essential growth. She returns repeatedly to simple meditations on the sayings of Jesus which yield food for thought and action now. She looks at a poem she wrote twenty years ago about the Samaritan woman at the well and is surprised that today she sees herself "a woman at the well of life—invited to face myself and my 'five men' (false idols? betrayals? substitution for Christian living? shallow diversions from firmer commitments?)."

She is committed to "Hanging In There" despite repeated frustrations and moments of anger at her own and other women's inability to share their gifts in parish life. Pondering the reasons for this dogged loyalty, she ultimately reaches the cross itself—that ultimate gift of human life for others. It is necessity, not merely tension, she now realizes, that causes misunderstanding and unjust suffering. Once she accepts that meaning in the cross, her faith becomes the source of life that deepens and extends her own growth.

The piety in these pages is human, one that grows in cooperation with life and nature. It strengthens the writer to reject the powerful idols of our culture: money, success and power, without regret. These contemporary golden calves are not easily rejected by those with conformist, cookie-cutter mentalities. Only the deep inner call to be responsible can liberate the one who hears it to the freedom of appreciating, not acquiring, this great, diverse creation.

The voice in this journal is truly "a different voice." In it head and heart, body, mind, and spirit are related. Unheard are the negative separations of our youth; yet discipline is present along with wonder and joy. In this journal we hear a feminine voice that is human. The author shares a daily pilgrimage with us at a time in her life when wit and wisdom enlighten her conversation. And in her concern to maintain relationships, make connections, and seek cooperation, the author embodies what new and "feminine" power researchers like Jean Baker Miller and Carol

Gilligan have identified as so long undervalued and so desperately needed if our world is to survive.

Not only does Marie McIntyre share with us, rather than lecture at us, she also acts as our representative. We must write our own "good news" in our lives, she tells us. We must live "the fifth gospel" today in this "now testament" time. And in her simple, faithful reflections on everything from "Snorkeling" and Hitchcock's *Lifeboat* to "Desolation," she shows us how to begin.

Sally Cunneen
West Nyack, New York

Contents

INTRODUCTION

***M**any of us who are female and Catholic in today's North American church find ourselves coping with discomfort. We live between the old and the new in a fast-moving society and a slowly-evolving church. Or is it the opposite?

Many of us find our voices still muted or muffled by structures that keep women "in their place"—namely a culturally conditioned situation of presumed service and silence. Because Catholic women are so often denied equal access to pulpit or podium, press or publishers, many turn to journal writing to express their feelings, thoughts, insights, and questions. As old diaries and new journals come to light, we discover the revelations of wisdom and truth which are quite often clear to women and obscure to men. Women do speak "in a different voice" and know "in a different way."

This book is simply a *pot pourri* of ideas and reflections of one woman whose lifestyle is middle class American and who reads a lot. Some of these reflections were written during times of joy; others respond to sorrow, frustration, fear, hope, and courage. Although the book speaks of both blessings and curses, it affirms some of the realities of life today for those of us who want to find and follow the Jesus who treated women as equals even in a culture which was conditioned against this honesty.

Although the reflections here are personal, limited, and conditioned by the time in which they were written, my hope is that they may stimulate more questions, better answers, and the courage to be ourselves.

1 Who Am I?

At a workshop on Christian education for adults, I copied down the phrase, "I am a song to be sung until my day is done." This seemed to me the self-definition of a person who lived in hope and was energized by the excitement of knowing that God is everywhere present and loving. It is a good definition because it is active. It shares joy. It speaks of total acceptance of life in a happy way.

It seems to me that this definition speaks of commitment, too—to keep singing no matter what. The mission is to "make music," that is, to bring joy to all around and to continue until the last moment. That leaves no time for despair or feeling sorry for one's self or turning away from people. Songs are sung for others even though the song must first be in the heart. But singing hearts are happy even when alone, alone but not lonely.

I wonder what definition I would write for myself if asked to do so now. A song? A word? A movement? A presence? Whatever the description, it somehow has to be in relationship to others. I cannot think of a word for total isolation other than a grave, and even "grave" is in relationship to time. Which reminds me: people can die before their time by giving up, by ceasing to be a song for others, or a word, or a presence.

"I am a song to be sung until my day is done." That's nice—even for people like me who can't sing very well. It is the trying that counts.

2 TURNING POINT

Every once in a while in life, one experiences an overall, undefinable awareness that something is beginning to be different. This ubiquitous awareness is difficult to name, but it signals a movement into a new phase of life, or consciousness, or it signals a need to take hold and make a stand or a firm decision.

It is a terrible time because it is so nebulous you can't define it, limit it, express it. You just know that you are "moving." And you also know that you don't know where you are moving to but you are frighteningly sure that you can't go back again.

One thinks of the image of "desert"—no person's land, no evident life, no directional signs. "Desert" played a real part in the life of Jesus, too. It was here that he came to decision, heard what he had to, and returned from "no place" to risk going into the future, willingly, accepting life totally and gratefully as the greatest gift of a loving-father-God.

Sometimes these turning points change from unfocused vagueness to specific clarity. We call them "calls" or "consciousness raising" or "teachable moments." At these awareness moments, we know that life is like a river—it continues to flow on, sometimes calmly, sometimes with a strong current, sometimes almost dry, sometimes flooding over.

The river analogy and the desert analogy help us at a turning-point-time to understand that life consists in going forward even when it is the vagueness or desert time prior to new insights and new life.

---

3 QUIET TIME

I am convinced that one of the most important needs in our culture today is "quiet time." If "quiet time" is enriched by the presence of good books or good art in its many forms, the result can be considered a very humanizing moment.

I had one of these gifts today. It came after a rush of company and a lot of emergency activity which was intensely energy-consuming. But when that quiet hour came, suddenly, the only demands on my time were my own work-addicted guilt feelings, and in the midst of this, I found a phrase or two to ponder.

I had been deeply concerned about the way I saw power being exercised in far too many situations. What I saw was the destruction of peoples' talents and emotions. I read a sentence in Charles W. Colson's *Loving God.* "The brighter I became, the more dangerous I was; the more power I acquired, the more power acquired me. I was blind."

This statement is truth in a nutshell. It is so easy to see this in others. In quiet time, I try to consider where my powers are and where my blindness is. It is amazing what new insights jump out when we center in quietly and intensely in this search for the truth about ourselves and our relations with others.

I know that I want my power to be the kind of power that is so often associated with women: cooperation, integration, affiliation, supportive networking, but I wonder if I ever come across as using or having power in an aggressive, demanding, manipulative way. This I dread. I find myself balking at people who use power in a tyrannical way, either overtly or in many of its covert forms. I need to search quietly and discover if I succumb to this form that I so resent in others. Sometimes the thing we hate the most in ourselves is what we first see in others—the mote and the beam!

I pray for the courage to be genuinely powerful in the sense of "being there for others" but not "being there just for me." So often in a crowd or at a party, the "being there for others" people are quietly present and sharing. The "being there for me" people turn the spotlight on themselves in a loud monologue which comes through as a crying need for attention because they do not feel loved enough or are unfulfilled in some real way. Yet the very "me first" demand and manipulation of others turns people away. The painful paradox has something to do with the way power is understood and used.

The patience of the "powerless" is often the real power that keeps things going, not the demands of the dictator at the top of the heap. The history of countries, organizations, parishes, and groups echoes this reality over and over again.

But what is difficult is that the "patience of the powerless" is quite often another phrase for unjust affliction, unequal distribution of opportunities, and a huge amount of suffering that the innocent must absorb in the hope that the real *shalom* of God will some day come to this world. It is this hope that gives the powerless their real power. It is in this trust that the real meaning of what Jesus said and did is so universally valid and that keeps making sense, no matter what.

During "quiet time" I actually hear that deep down truth emerging from those guts of mine which were anointed in baptism/confirmation. It is that truth which tells me that striving to be Jesus-like in today's world is the only way to go. "I am the way, the truth, and the life" continues to be meaningful in new ways each day.

No wonder I need quiet time! How terrifyingly easy it is to forget and lose one's way, one's truth, and one's life!

---

4 DOUBT AND HOPE

It struck me one day that the very last words Jesus said before he died expressed the human condition in a truly universal way: "Why have you forsaken me?" "I commend my spirit into your hands."

That is *doubt* and *hope* in a nutshell. While he cried out that he was forsaken, he ended with "I give myself to you."

It seems to me that we face this dilemma each day of our lives. We live in doubt as the other side of faith. Somehow, we want to trust in a loving God "out there" and yet we so often feel the absence of any sign of that presence.

It is probably when the doubt is the greatest that hope is the only answer. Perhaps that is why people in third world countries who are exploited and unjustly dominated by others seem to endure with a consistent cry of hope on their lips. It is all they have.

I have always felt that *hope* is the energizer that keeps us going in the right direction, even when we cannot see ahead, even when we cry "Why have you forsaken me?" There is something deep down inside of us that knows that life calls out to life, that hope is trust in a living God who knows and loves us even though we don't know how. Where there is no hope, there is no life.

Perhaps that is what resurrection is all about — the bursting forth of hope and new life in the midst of destruction and death and apparent hopelessness (lifelessness).

At any rate, I'm grateful to Jesus for his last words. They help me to know that he has been there and that it is all right. When I cry out in the pain of being forsaken, I know he knows. When I echo "Into thy hands, I commend my spirit," I know I am in a warm place. I know my trust will lead me to inner peace and gratitude-joy.

There is something about gratitude-joy that banishes doubt. Gratitude-joy is the breeding place for hope.

5 THINKING WITH THE HEART

One of the most exciting things I can do when I feel beleaguered is to STOP and pick up the Bible. There is always a treasure, a treat, a surprise waiting.

Yesterday, I read some of the marvelous passages in the book of Ecclesiastes and came across the phrase "thinking with the heart."

What a wonderful world we would live in if we knew how to "think with the heart." We would begin by placing ourselves in the other person's shoes and trying to see the world from that vantage point. We would temper our theories by the practical reality that only "thinking with the heart" can reveal. We would begin to think with *under*standing and not *over*standing as is the temptation when we operate from the eyebrows up.

But that was just one of the wonderful phrases to be found in wisdom and proverb literature in the Hebrew Scriptures. All these wise sayings have come out of lives lived with time for contemplation, lives spent communicating in the oral tradition that honed sayings into gems which now sparkle guidance to anyone who finds them.

What if the entire continent's people had to begin each day with just ten minutes of Wisdom, Proverbs,

Sirach, Solomon ...? What if we fed on these truths instead of watching shallow news stories on TV that make so many murderers and thieves and liars into our media heroes? What if each of us were to carry around in our hearts, mantra-like, one such gem each day? What difference would it make? Perhaps I should find out for myself. Today it will be this one:

> "A glad heart is excellent medicine
> a spirit depressed wastes the bones away."
>
> (Proverbs 17:22)

6 Fear

A very loving and discerning priest once told me he believed that the greatest evil in the world is fear. The fears of people keep them from becoming whole and, therefore, impede the coming of the kingdom of trust and love.

People fear the truth about themselves and about others. People fear the frail thread that connects them to life temporarily and to one another with fragile ties. Thus, fear freezes people into immobility, into states of depression where despair is the only horizon, where there is no hope. And without hope, there is no future and no life.

I see this fear in the eyes of people who scream at other people. I see this terrible fear manifested in envies and jealousies because others have been more gifted somehow. I see this fear in the silence of people who are paid to say "yes." I hear this fear in the circumlocution of people who feel their jobs will be jeopardized if they say what they really think.

Thus, fear does make cowards of us all. This is a double bind, because cowards rarely conquer evil, and fear is evil.

And yet, Jesus tells us, "Be not afraid. I go before you. Come, follow me and I will bring you rest."

The example of Jesus is certainly not the example of a fearful person. His "fear of Yahweh" was awesome respect, not fear in the sense of groveling. Instead, he had the courage to say out loud what he thought of some of the Pharisees—"brood of vipers," "painted sepulchers." Strong words describing the inauthentic, the hypocritical. And what did that kind of courage get him? Crucifixion.

Is crucifixion the sacrament of courage? Does one have to die each time a truth is uttered? Does being called to "new life" mean the courage to live "beyond the lie?"

Do all the seven "deadly sins" have their manifestation in some form of fear? Of course! Fear is the sacrament of the seven deadly sins.

Lord, take away our fears by helping us to admit our sins.

7 False Idols

Discovering a great book is like finding the pearl of great price. Even though I love Donald Evans' *Struggle and Fulfillment,* I don't seem to find the time to ponder its truths often enough. Yet today, while reflecting on his chapter on "Fidelity and Idolatry," I realized how so many of our problems come from a lack of really understanding how often we substitute the state of idolatry for the life of fidelity and therefore are forever ill at ease.

If "idolatry is fostered by the repression of anxiety" as Evans says, then it is no wonder that we have so many false idols in our culture which is permeated by the anxiety we promote by creating more and more idols. The vicious circle keeps us so dizzy there seems little chance of finding a clear-headed space to stop and look at the "sanctity of givenness" in the first place. Maybe this need for silent space is why retreat houses are so full these days, and people are clamoring for spiritual gurus and guides.

Evans quotes a sentence from Martin Buber's *I and Thou*, which I should find and read again now that I'm two decades older and wiser than when I first read it. Buber says, "Whoever is dominated by the idol whom he wants to acquire, have, and hold, possessed by his desire to possess, can find a way to God only by returning, which involves a change not only of the goal, but also of the kind of movement . . ." Wow! Beautiful Buber echoes Jesus who says it differently: "He who saves his life will lose it in the end."

It is so exciting to realize that when one struggles in the search for truth, one can find paradox everywhere, and that great minds come out of their own time and cultures and emerge toward the light that brightens others with similar insights into the human condition. Buber calls for a return. . .a change not only of the goal, but also of the kind of movement. Jesus calls for a "change of heart," a *metanoia*. But doesn't heart mean the whole person?

How do I discover what idols I'm chasing and how do I return from the chase in order to find God? Evans tells me that "fidelity involves the courage to allow one's anxiety to emerge into consciousness instead of repressing it and replacing it by idolatry." I can understand that for others more easily than for myself. I tell my discouraged and despairing Catholic women friends to "go trust their own guts" instead of putting themselves into situations where clerical schizophrenia may violate their own rights and frustrate their need for a community of affirmation. I can tell them to save themselves by staying away from what, sadly, deals more death to them than life. Yet, I understand the pain and the paradox because, in my own guts, I go through the same torture.

So what idol have we put in the way of fidelity to the sanctity of our own giveness or intrinsic being? Have we substituted without question the idolization of a human being by giving another "power" to decide and choose what we ourselves are called to decide and choose as authentic adults? Have we built around our idol a building, an institution, a liturgy, a dogmatic proclamation, a code (of Canon Law—something that you have to ignore a lot of to be sure), all in our attempt to have a Linus blanket, a security symbol? If we do this and this and this, we shall be saved? Saved . . .?

In our church, we are preached at to support the annual parish festival as our means of unity, our common bond, our proof of loyalty. This idol calls us to eat a lot, sell a lot of junk to one another, acquire someone else's non-essentials, etc., all in the name of paying the *idol's* bills and keeping the idol in front of us as a security ticket to someplace else because what we have is not the answer. What is so terrible about this blindness is that the people who are manipulated into believing there is a kind of virtue in this wild circus have never been shown the beauty that lies behind the idol. We are all people of the idol or "people of the lie," as Scott Peck puts it, when we do not help one another to turn back and have a change of direction and a change of heart.

But here I go—seeing the need for group change and not asking myself how I must, myself, turn from my need for security and be open to the surprises of beauties and challenges of each day which I cannot program or control.

God, let me see and hear what you are revealing in the little things: "A little child shall lead them," "the clowns of God," "power in weakness," "small is beautiful," "consider the lilies of the field." What IF we REALLY considered the lilies of the field and lived with fidelity to perpetual openness to rain and shine, cold and heat, joy and sorrow, cross and crown, peace and war, love and hate, truth and lie, ecstasy and disillusionment, friends and foes, black and white, night and day, and above all "being finite" in the face of the Infinite?

8 SEPARATE AND TOGETHER

When I look around at the lives of many married people, I wonder why it is that we seem to live out our lives doing so many superficial things together and so many meaningful things apart. Is it possible that we are permanently individuals and that marriage, no matter how close, will never meld us into "one being"?

How many married people find that they are truly able to share with their partner what is really meaningful in their lives? We share the common courtesies; we enjoy common entertainments; we play the same games sometimes. Yet, how many people get close enough to the person they say they love to reveal themselves, their dreams, their real desires, their hopes? Are we afraid that we will be rejected? Can we not trust enough to feel that we will be accepted?

I know a couple who have promised themselves a half day a week together, and in spite of their individual and different jobs and their children at home, they do manage this priority in their lives. They struggle to communicate who they really are to one another. What I have seen happening as a result is that an integrated sexuality is emerging. He has learned a female sensitivity to others. She has learned a less dependent trust in her job. Together, they have learned to listen to others. When they are in a group, they are the antennae into which messages flow and are received with quiet understanding. What seems to happen is that the more they reveal themselves to one another, the better able they are to turn and help and listen and comfort and understand others. Their own giving becomes their better mode for receiving.

I see this couple as a model of what should happen in marriage, and yet I also see that they have their personal struggles. In the self-revelations, they have come to understand how "yet separate" they are and how they are called to do different things in the world because they have been gifted with different talents. They have learned to accept this and still leave space for the other without domination or smothering. They affirm one another's gifts and take pride in them. They model energy and joy as a result.

For them, even though they have to do a lot of "superficial things together," they are also learning not to do meaningful things only when they are apart. And that makes all the difference.

9 EQUAL WOMEN AND MEN

Yesterday a male colleague asked a friend if she ever wanted to get married again. She said, "No." It perplexed him, but it helped him come to an understanding that women are not necessarily made to find their fulfillment and happiness in a man. The attitudes of this culture had deceived him. He was just beginning to observe that many women he knew were content to be autonomous and even single parents.

When I heard this, I reflected on how much joy women have in the company of women. Statistics tell us that there are several million widows in the U.S. over the age of 65. Many of these women are content "to be" and, in proportion to their own independence and skills, do not seem to need a companion who is male, although they do need companions.

In a sense, as men become more aware that women can be autonomous, particularly when there is financial justice, men become less sure of themselves and their roles in the world. The gnawingness of this knowledge creates an ill-at-easeness that manifests itself in unnecessary defensiveness and turf protection that eventually boomerangs.

In the business world, more and more intelligent and competent women threaten men, and men react in tragically fruitless ways. They do not seem to understand that competent women are not necessarily seeking their jobs or seeking to dominate them. Most women are happy working with, not working above or working below, but rather working as equals in a way that should not threaten anyone.

"In the kingdom of God," Jesus said, "there is neither male nor female." Would that it could be so in the world of business and in the world of church, and in any world where groups of either sex gather to be grateful for the gift of life.

10 The Need To Be Alone

It was a blue day today. When one feels so low that going out to others is too energy-demanding, one turns inward in a kind of immobility that causes exhaustion, dullness, and an inability to do anything. If this occurs on a Sunday when a person is normally called to public communal worship, the dilemma is great.

Today I knew I could not cope. Today I knew that an attempt at public worship would be a charade; yet, I needed Jesus. I needed him alone. I needed to hear him tell me about myself without the distraction of a kind of vulgar approach to liturgy where most people understood not what the so-called symbols were speaking and therefore left the experience untouched and unchanged.

So I went to a quiet corner in the house and played some dramatic records of the life of Jesus, beginning with the sermon on the mount. I know these are not Jesus' sayings "all-at-once-in-one-sermon-and-one-place," but rather a collection that the redactors of Matthew's gospel put together, but I had to listen and listen and hear and hear and learn and accept. Then I listened to the parables, the stories, and then about his suffering and death.

So very many truths were revealed to me in this quiet morning, this self-imposed retreat, this delightful and needed oasis in the overwhelming confusion I often find in my life.

I began to think about how women cope in a patriarchal and militaristic world, and I realized that it is something like Upstairs/Downstairs. Upstairs, the men compete, step on one another and make wars. Downstairs, the women bandage wounds, soothe, heal, and console. Women survive by making networks of interlocking relationships. Women, indeed, *have* community every day.

Men, on the other hand, for the most part, are conditioned to live and work in a competitive society where "up the ladder" means lonely isolation, where the other climber on the same rung is to be pushed off or treated with suspicion. Men live with psychological isolation daily.

Is it possible, then, that the Sunday liturgy is a man's need more than a woman's? Is it possible that the "meaninglessness" women complain about after Sunday celebrations is saying something we haven't faced? Is it possible that men need community but can't admit it so they create liturgical forms that help to fill the void in their lives? But women who network all week long often find that a retreat into quiet time, their own corner, a peaceful "being alone with the God within" is what they need.

I suppose that people would then ask why it is that the majority of Sunday worshippers are women. Perhaps this raises another question. It is also true that the case is not "either/or," and so perhaps there need to be many more far better questions.

How do we really worship God—with symbol systems that were better understood in another era and for another people? With references to biblical truths and events that are not part of the common heritage of the people gathered to listen? With symbols that are not explained? With power plays behind the human scene that jockey only men into the pulpit to continue proclaiming the good news according to a man's vision but rarely a woman's? No doubt this half-revelation creates the schizophrenia all about us and we feel "half there" instead of "whole" and holy.

The questions continue to come. Maybe some day, so will the answers, particularly if we refocus our understanding of "who" and "where" God really is.

11 ANGER

The phone rang. It was Mary with a marvelous quote she wanted to share from her reading: "Scratch a woman's psyche deep enough and you find a thousand years of anger."

The interesting thing is that Mary and I both knew what that meant. Upon reflection I realized I had noted an increasingly large number of books and articles on the subject of anger recently. Publishers who had ignored such a topic were now producing books on anger. It seems to me that it is all coming together. As the emerging consciousness of women meets the freedom of information in an open milieu, women are coming up for air and taking a new look at the subtle and not-so-subtle hierarchical forms of their western culture and realizing that their anger is the genuine expression of repression and suppression.

The great proliferation of women's presses are producing books that include diaries, research into the past centuries, balancing the biases of recorded history, etc., so that all of us are coming to grips with the truth that our world's institutions have been designed by men to keep men in power and women in a form of slave state. Paradoxically the very men who say they are not sexist because of their financial generosity to the women in their lives fail to begin to comprehend that they can smother their women in material luxuries but destroy their spirits at the same time. That is probably why so many economically comfortable women (who shouldn't have any gripes) are the most angry.

This whole "thousand years of anger" is what the American Catholic woman is being asked to cope with and is in a double bind about. She does not want this anger to destroy her as she affirms life. But her energies are dissected as she strives to ignore the sapping of her strength in unjust clerical situations while she works to bring new life into church organizations and committees.

Probably, intelligent women on parish councils where the main mode of operation is "Yes, Father" are the women who suffer the most. They know the difference. They know they are called to freedom and equality both by the very fact of their humanity and their baptism. They know that the "Yes, Father" structure is not only a cop-out, it is a violation of the ecumenical insights of the council that met over a quarter of a century ago and specifically declared in its *Constitution on the Church* and its more challenging *Gaudium et Spes* that all are called to bring about the kingdom where God's justice reigns.

Yes, "scratch a woman's psyche deep enough and you find a thousand years of anger." It's true. It's sad. What is sadder is that she may have to endure that anger for another thousand years. Which is more painful? Under the surface or out in the open?

12 Pilate's Courageous Wife

The other day I came across one of the gems to be found every time we open the Bible. This one sparkled out of the scene where Pontius Pilate was washing his hands of responsibility for the death of Jesus. It is not hard for cowards to do this—use a symbol or an excuse to keep the *status quo* intact even though the voice of conscience cries otherwise.

Pilate admitted that he found no cause to condemn Jesus but he gave in to the rabble rousers, the mob which was threatened by the goodness personified in Jesus. It mirrored back to them what they did not want to see in themselves, and so they had to crack this mirror. They had to get rid of this reflection. And Pilate "washed his hands." Hands are made for serving and helping, and washing is made for cleansing. Pilate used these symbols sacrilegiously, so the opposites occurred.

But the gem I began to talk about. . .it was the voice of Pilate's wife. How dare she come into his man's world and cry out in an attempt to stop the injustice! What was she doing on man's turf where law and order meant being politically expedient? Pilate's wife had a dream.

I know that dreams are used in the Bible as modes of communication, as methods of revelation. Pilate's wife dreamed about the goodness and innocence of Jesus and the truth had to be shared, shouted, cried out before it was too late.

Matthew tells us that Pilate knew that "it was out of jealousy" that Jesus had been handed over to him (a human enough emotion from the powerbrokers in the presence of genuine power). Then Matthew says, "Now as he was seated in the chair of judgment, his wife sent him a message: 'Have nothing to do with that man. I have been upset all day by a dream I had about him (Matthew 26:42).'"

"Upset all day" is a phrase many women will readily understand. She pondered and sifted the evidence and knew that Jesus should not be standing before the judgment seat. So, after being "upset all day," she finally got up the courage to trespass into the ruling world of Rome and cry out in an innocent man's defense.

Was she a failure? Two thousand years later, we know she tried. Her voice gives hope to all women who cry out against injustice and pride of status and the human weakness of men who "wash their hands" of their responsibility to seek, not order, but justice.

Pilate's wife gets a small line in Matthew's gospel—almost a footnote in small type, but it is a little gem that sparkles out of Scripture and gives those of us who are "upset all day" the courage to speak out.

There is so much more to this event. One could write a book about it, but for now it is good to know that two thousand years ago a woman, probably uprooted from her native Rome, spoke the truth in a land dominated by a foreign power. Even though she appeared to be part of that domination, she courageously spoke the truth, and that truth has been proclaimed around the world, because truth by its essence is beyond time, locale, and space. "And the truth shall set you free."

This little gem that sparkles for me in the Bible lights a way for me and for all women in dominating societies. Proclaim the truth. Many are, thank God, and perhaps when the chorus is loud enough we will be heard and innocent people will be free and there will be peace on earth.

13 A Cunning Crown

It was just a phrase, but I've remembered it: "A cunning crown for Jesus." Sometimes adjectives make us stop short and see and hear for the first time.

We may take "a crown of thorns" for granted because we have heard the expression so many times, but when someone says "a cunning crown for Jesus," we have to stop and ask what this could mean.

The painful points that penetrate into the one human head the world honors as containing the revelation of God seem like an attack on truth coming from many sources. The tangled bramble branch with its steel-like thorns was fashioned in a moment of drunken madness by a common soldier and forced on Jesus. Then he was ridiculed as a king with a crown.

Perhaps this is the great symbol of human evil—that the insensitive and unaware part of us symbolized in the drunken soldier is free to try to deface and destroy all that stands for human goodness, truth, beauty, and love. No wonder Jesus had to cry, "Forgive them, for they know not what they do."

"A cunning crown" indeed. There is something about "cunning" that stands for a twisting of the truth, just as the thorny branch was twisted. The dictionary defines "cunning" as sly, crafty, or skillful in deception. So it is a good word to describe a crown that was made for a "king" who was not a king in this world's common usage. And, paradoxically, it was a cunning crown in another sense. Didn't the drunken soldier who sought to appear clever in the eyes of his peers fashion a crown that *is* symbolic of anyone who attempts to be savior in the world? Don't all saviors have to suffer, have to feel the pain of rejection, misunderstanding, the burden of anguish encircling them from many sources simultaneously?

"A cunning crown for Jesus"—yes! But the more I think of it, the more I understand that the meaning under the symbols we find in the Bible reveals truth to us so much more than the surface words.

I need to remember, when my own burden of anguish seems too exquisite to bear, that he who modeled the crown for the first time also modeled the response: "Father, forgive them, for they know not what they do."

14 HANGING IN THERE

Yesterday I cried in church because my emotions were touched at a level I had never understood before. The sermon was about "hanging in there." The pastor, who is a skilled counselor, was universalizing on the theme so necessary for all the hurting people who were confiding in him. He kept repeating that "hanging in there" and making the most of our present surroundings and relationships is what we are called to do. He noted that 75 percent of the people who ran away from a painful situation, particularly in marriage, found, after a ten-year period, that it was not any better elsewhere. Only one in four said it was better.

As I was struggling with the "hanging in there" question myself, the sermon was particularly grace-filled for me and I felt it was a blessing to be in church hearing this word.

But it was when we sang the final hymn that reflected on Jesus "hanging in there" until he hung on the cross that I realized the terrible extent of Jesus' real psychological and emotional suffering. Perhaps this was even greater than the already awful physical suffering. Then I realized that this example given us who call ourselves Christians "stuck it out" until it killed him; but it was in his total giving that new life was possible for the rest of us.

Yesterday, for the first time possibly, I understood that when I pray to be like Jesus I pray for crucifixion ultimately. How can an *Abba* call this "the way to go"?

It is when these questions come that I know I'm surrounded by superficial answers and that it is in quiet prayer and meditation that I will get to the deeper and more revealing level.

Jesus hanging on the cross has an entirely new meaning for me. The contradiction of the cross—vertical and horizontal—has a new meaning today. I've always seen it as a symbol of tension, but now I see it as a symbol of necessity. Paradoxically, it IS the eastern yin/yang intrinsically together.

The old crusaders had a motto in Latin that meant, "In this sign thou shalt conquer." It *is* the sign that conquers when we think about it enough. No wonder the cross has meant so much to so many people through the centuries. Probably the poets have preserved the greatest insight here. There is no Christianity without the cross. There is no life in an empty cross. What makes the cross the ultimate sign and reality of salvation is the *kenosis* that takes place on it. The gift of human life. . ."hanging in there."

Grant us, Lord, the strength to "hang in there" on our little crosses if, in the process, we can save others. Even when we cannot save ourselves.

"Come down from the cross," the bigwigs of this world jeered at the feet of Jesus. "Look—he saves others. He cannot save himself!"

What difference would it have made in the world if Jesus had come down? And Gandhi? And Martin Luther King? And Florence Nightingale? And Dorothy Day? And all the people I admire most?

And me?

15 Mary as Model

One of the best and clearest paragraphs I've read about Mary I found on page 940 in the St. Andrew Bible Missal. It was written as an introduction for the feast of the Assumption which seems to have its origins around the fifth century.

The paragraph reads: "Her real greatness lies more in her faith, which caused her first to conceive in her heart, even before conceiving in her womb (Augustine). 'Blest is she who trusted,' first in the announcement made to her by the angel Gabriel, but also in the whole adventure which it implied. For a vocation is always a discovery. Mary was continually challenged to renew, to broaden, to deepen the act of faith asked of her in Nazareth. Her vocation led to the foot of the cross. There the true greatness of her faith was revealed. There her song of praise took on new depth. Thus she became the model of believers. Her assumption into the fullness of life is hope for all."

What struck me most about that paragraph is the reality that "a vocation is always a discovery," and that we too are continually challenged to renew, broaden, and deepen our faith. But also that this faith ultimately leads to the cross. There is no other path if it is to be "the road well taken," "the way" of the *Way.*

Mary is the model of believers because she gave Jesus to the world and went with him to the cross and, because of this, we can say that her assumption into the fullness of life is hope for all.

My image of "assumption into fullness of life" is far different today than it was in my childhood, but my understanding of no fullness without relenting hope and trust is also something I did not know as a child.

Many women are discovering Mary in a new way. Not as a plaster statue of sweetness and passive submission, but rather as a woman who faced and accepted reality with calm perseverance.

When I think of Mary today, I see her as a marvelous model to imitate in a far more demanding way than when, two decades ago, I thought of her as an intercessor or bridge to Jesus. "All for Jesus through Mary" was the motto that loomed large in my life at that time. Today it is more like "Mary, model to be imitated for trusting hope, perseverance, and 'being there when needed.'"

Perhaps this is best summed up in the declarative sentence from Luke 11:28 in the gospel for August 15: *Blessed are they who hear the word of God and keep it.*

What an accolade! What a profound truth! What a demanding challenge! What a liberating insight!

I thank Mary for being Mary. I hope that some day, in some way, someone will be able to say of me, "Thank her for being her."

16 COPING

This is one of those days when my body tingles with an unnatural apprehension or fatigue or fugue-ness. I find it difficult to calm down inside, and every "little job" becomes a mountain. What should take a minute looks like an hour's task.

I long for time out for a retreat, time out from the permanently constant demands from people around me to "do this," "do that," and "do this" again, much of which is one-way service to the other or something that is less than intelligent. I suppose I could do it all if I could put my mind aside, but I can't. I sometimes wonder if people who have gone senile have gone that route as a biological escape from painful situations.

Today the word is COPING. Coping with the next demand, the next conversation, the next task of organizing for the next demand, the next conversation, and the next task. I need a retreat. I need an oasis in the desert. I need to get calm inside again. Yet, all the loose ends seem so entangling! I understand why people escape through alcohol or dull TV or cheap fiction. I also understand that escape is never the solution.

I need the inner quiet of Jesus today. I need to hear him say, "These things will pass away, but my words will never pass away."

"I *am* the way. I *am* the truth. I *am* the life."

17 Preferring Our Prisons

It is always amazing to me to discover how much truth there is in the Bible that we miss on the first reading. There is a story in chapter 5 of Mark's gospel about a Gerasene demoniac who lived among the tombs. He was a prisoner of his own mental instability, of being a social outcast, of being ostracized by his co-religionists. Yet, when he saw Jesus, he asked to be left alone. He didn't want to escape from his environment, ugly as it was. "The demon we know is usually safer than the demon we do not know."

It wasn't until I read a commentary on this event by Sr. Patricia Smith, RSM, that I realized what I had missed in this scene. In a way, it is an analogy of our own lives when we prefer to stay prisoner to something evil, ugly, inhuman rather than accept Jesus' call to conversion, to change, to become someone better and freer. We too are often afraid of change. We too often tell Jesus to go away. Leave us alone! We like our prison, hateful and constricting as it is.

The event, as described by Mark, tells us about the reaction of the neighbors when the outcast *is* delivered of his devils. *They* were filled with fear. They didn't know what to make of him now that he was normal. They were more comfortable with him when he was predictably insane.

This is so often the case when we move into being what we have not been before. Women in the church who have been unassertive, quietly accepting the role of non-equal in the structure in spite of Jesus's teaching and example, discover how violently men react when they stand up for equality. Men, who fear the "competition" of women (never understanding that women want cooperation, not competition), react by cutting off the possibilities for women as much as possible. Of course, this human/inhuman reaction always backfires, but it *is* what women do experience in many, many cases.

And how we react when a friend or an acquaintance does the courageously right thing? Do we resent her growth into holiness and wholeness because it tells us that we haven't changed or moved out of our own little familiar prisons?

I must meditate on Mark 5:1-20 again—and again—and again! And then, instead of telling Jesus to go away, I must ask him to help me go with him.

18 HAPPINESS IN COMMITMENT

Sometimes I wonder if researchers come up with a lot of new information or merely confirm what the experience of living has taught us. A couple of years ago, I read about a Gallup Poll report on religion in America which showed that the happiest people are those who are highly committed, particularly in some sector of American religious life. The report ended with the statement that "the highly committed express general happiness and satisfaction in family life, in relationship to others, and many consider they live to a degree of happiness far above average."

That, of course, does not surprise anyone who has been alive for a few years and has observed the human scene. The final paragraph in the report I found totally redundant:

"These findings seriously challenge the prevalent view in our society that wealth, power, and self-indulgence are the keys to happiness and personal satisfaction."

The terrible unrest, violence, and anxiety which results from a "gimme" culture is so much a part of us that we may miss this "very air we breathe." When we step outside of it and into a society, a milieu, a country, or some place where giving and sharing and loving and being-for-one-another are more of a way of life, we find joy and trust and love and creative living.

On the personal level, I meditate on Jesus teaching us that if we try to save our lives we lose them, and if we try to lose them, we save them. This, to me, is the obvious kernel of truth that I must make my own day by day. But some days it is difficult. We need to be with a giving person to help the giving grow in us. "Gimme" people tighten us up, make us resentful, aggressive, and ultimately mean.

Let my commitment be to giving as much as possible and especially when it seems almost impossible. Here, I will ultimately find my internal and true joy, I will know that I have been true to the core truth that Jesus expressed with his own life. Being near to Jesus, then, is the need I have to be near a giving person who will help me to be a giver.

19 TOTAL CONTRADICTION

Sometimes I get carried away. I get excited over poetic phrases—words strung together by a Shakespeare or a Gerard Manley Hopkins, or a forgotten or unnamed truth teller. At other times, it's the cold logic put into one screamingly intelligent sentence that gets me going. I want to stop and frame the sentence and send it to everyone I know and don't know. I want the whole world to read it.

I recently copied a sentence of the second type. In an article entitled "Moral Confusion in the Nuclear Age," (*Christian Century*, April 4, 1984) Justus George Lawler says, "It is ontologically impossible to intend to use something in order not to use it." This sentence is powerful, I think, revealing what muddled thinking is behind the drive to accumulate nuclear weapons. Yet, I have friends who would ignore the truth and say we are "building bombs to protect democracy." They dare to use terms that they do not understand. We speak what we do not know. A nuclear bomb is not a protection. It is an annihilation. Democracy *per se* is an ideal hard to find anywhere. I try to think of an analogy that would put Lawler's sentence into everyday experience in our church and I come up with these few thoughts:

"It is ontologically impossible to intend a liturgy which celebrates gratitude for all life in a community of people who spend their lives building instruments of mass annihilation."

"It is ontologically impossible to intend to cook for a family in order not to let the members of the family eat."

"It is ontologically impossible to be authentic in our relationship to God if we think we must worship only according to specified rubrics laid down by others."

It is ontologically impossible to call the church the people of God when the context means "some of the people."

For me, it is ontologically impossible to celebrate thanksgiving in public when the prayer says that Jesus died for *us men* and our salvation (even though I know this was not in the original text and its deletion has been ordered).

20 Our Shaped Way of Knowing

Someone said, "The cookie cutter in your head says what you are going to get." I guess that is another way of validating the suggestion that we can and do shape our own futures.

This saying warns me that the very way my mind works probably shapes my expectations and hopes. What difference in shaping, then, between the optimist and the pessimist! The saying also helps me understand that if I know the shape of the cookie cutter in someone else's head, I know what I am going to get.

I have listened to priests whose cookie cutter was shaped by several years of seminary training that gave them a vision of a triumphant church—a vision that they had all the truth, and that as ordained specialists they even had it in their own cookie cutters. So they judge the world and its people by how their cookie cutter was formed. For many of them, the way they saw things made them wary of women, and deprived them of being open to other than scholastic philosophical forms which might undergird the way they thought about God. When I understand that this is the way they think, I can also understand how very difficult it is for them to hear me who has not had that shaping of the cookie cutter. I understand that I will not be heard or understood, and that I have to find a different way to make contact. Using the words they memorized as having special meanings will not help me at all. When he became pope, Pope Paul VI made an urgent plea for dialogue. When? When?

21 THE GOD OF THE BIBLE

"The God of the Bible is the God of the poor and oppressed." This sentence jumps out at me with a brand new meaning when I realize that God may be another name for hope. All poor and oppressed peoples need a relationship of hope for survival. Otherwise, why bother? Why not die?

In a classic old movie, "Lifeboat," the frustrated survivors of a German attack which sinks their ship finally kill the one German in their lifeboat. The single man who did not take part in the mob murder, motivated by prejudice, frustration, and revenge, was the black man who knew Psalm 22 by heart and who turned to God (or at least looked upward toward "heaven") when survival looked bleak and the people in the lifeboat did not know where to turn.

The black man stood apart from the mass murder. Was it because of his transcendent hope or his transcendent knowledge based on that hope, understood experientially, that kept him from being "a little less than the angels" as someone defined the meaning of being human?

What was obvious in that fascinating Hitchcock film was how little the mighty and the powerful felt a need for a power beyond themselves, for a relationship that was more humanizing and fulfilling than their present life styles. One survivor depended on his money and power of authority. One depended on her talent as a writer and photographer who surveyed the human scene without getting too involved in it. One put his trust in Rosie who really was not there for him at all but gave him the feeling of value and reason for living anyway. One drifted on the whims of other people's decisions for his life. One was in love with the wrong person and could not find a way out of her depression. One was a highly ambitious egotist born on the "wrong side," looking to the glitter of the "right side" for fulfillment and success and reason for living.

All the people who merged together to murder the German sea captain had unfulfillments and needs which were not being met. Somehow, they were all hollow as humans.

As each entered the lifeboat they were individualistic, self-centered, isolated from one another. Paradoxically, as they were stripped of their powers, their ego-supporters, what emerged was their need to work together for survival. They began to relate to one another in a more human and caring way.

By the time the rescue ship was on the horizon, they all had been stripped down to the bareness of bodies needing food and water. In the process of this stripping down, they all had to let go of something important to them. For the most part, the letting go was not freely done, but came about through the forces of nature and the carelessness or self-centeredness of their companions.

And when the rescue ship finally takes them aboard, out of the chaos of death-dealing water into the new life represented by life-giving water, food, clothing, and a new beginning, one wonders if these survivors will see life differently? Will they be "born again," or will that seeming intrinsic instinct of "an eye for an eye," a "killing for a killing," stay with them? Will they return to their ego-support systems or will they have learned that letting go is twice possessing?

Will they, this motley collection of humankind, ever come to know what the wise man knew as he prayed Psalm 22 from the heart? ". . .for I am with you all the days. . . ."

As I reread, "The God of the Bible is the God for the poor and oppressed," I know once again what the poor and oppressed black man knew from experience, namely, that human nature left to itself is ultimately destructive. We all need to "reach out and touch someone" who *is* the power of hope for us that transcends our limitedness and finiteness.

The God of the Bible is the God for the poor and oppressed. That means, in a million ways, the he/she God of the Bible is the God for us all.

22 THE FIFTH GOSPEL

How long does a person have to live before the truth comes through that we write our own "good news" story as we go through life? How long before we realize that

Matthew, Mark, Luke, and John wrote about Jesus as they understood him to be and that we must do likewise?

Matthew's gospel tells of the Jesus who is the new Moses, the fulfillment of the prophecies and longings for a Messiah in the Hebrew Scriptures. Mark's gospel pictures for us the human Jesus more than the later gospels which were written when people began to reflect more on "the divinity" of Jesus. Luke, the gentile, had a tenderness and understanding of women and social justice; John's writing is contemplative, double-visioned like a poet who sees beneath or beyond the surface.

All of these versions of Jesus attract us and we probably find ourselves drawn more to one than the other, depending on our own personality. Each gospel account is like the piece of a puzzle, all necessary to see the total picture. Yet the four pieces do not complete the picture of Jesus for me.

I'm the missing piece.

My story must be written, too. People who hear me say I am Christian must find a gospel account of Jesus in my life. They have to hear and see my words and actions that speak and show that I know and love the Jesus who has shown us his God, a loving person and not mere creative force. . .

. . .who has taught us that we are part of the whole (Whatsoever you do to others, you do to me)

. . .who values integrity and truth

. . .who lives with the pilgrim and the poor (and has no where to lay his head)

. . .who relates equally to men, women, sinners, saints

. . .who has the courage and discernment to fight temptation to passing glory, power, prestige. . .

. . .who encourages us to seek the better part, to be fully integrated, alive. . .

. . .et cetera

When I think of myself as the fifth gospel, as the word made flesh in me, now, to be the revelation of Jesus to others, I am suddenly confronted with the responsibility of it all!

What if I had been baptized and confirmed not in the hazy mist of infancy and childhood, but today—NOW?

What if I begin to understand that my mandate in life, my *raison d'etre* is to be a living fifth gospel? How shall I write it? Where do I begin?

Matthew and Luke felt the need to begin Jesus' story with infancy narratives that have a mythic quality. Mark begins with Jesus as adult, on the threshold of his chief work. John goes back to pre-existence, looking into the mind of God for beginnings.

And where do I begin?

I think I begin with today because this is all I have. My today is the pinnacle of all my yesterdays, yes, but it is today that I understand that I am the fifth gospel.

Today, now in the silence of a "home retreat hour," I see and hear the call to ever remember my gift of life is for being gospel in my space and time.

So, though it may be Chapter 60 in chronology, today is Chapter 1 in my fifth gospel. Today I begin again and in a new way to be Jesus for others.

What a new vision this gives, a new strength, a new security, a new willingness, a new understanding and joy/terror/joy that is the call to divinity—to total human integrity, complete *kenosis*, and therefore, the marvelous mystery and paradox of defeat/victory.

Today, I begin again. Body of Christ. Amen.

23 PAIN

One of the most perceptive writers of this last half of the 20th century was William Stringfellow, a small man whose body gave him permanent pain but who had a will to fight the dismal and destructive forces of this constant companion of his.

He ends his best book written just before his death in 1985, *The Politics of Spirituality* (Westminster Press) with a profound statement: "Pain is a true mystery. . .yet it is known that pain is intercessory: one is never alone in pain but is always a surrogate of everyone else who hurts—which is categorically everybody."

In all probability, anyone who has suffered a great deal, physically, emotionally, or intellectually, will need no further clarification of that insight. So often we try to turn mysteries into problems to be solved, thinking that we can order, classify, box up, and put an end to such things, that we can conquer them with our deeper knowledge helped by new technology.

It is those who truly suffer who come to know that there is no such thing as modifying a mystery and shrinking it into a problem. The mystery of evil in the world, of "unjust" pain, of unfair suffering of the "good" has been with us since the dawn of history and will remain because it is the genius of God that knows the necessity of this mystery for the realization and divinization of humanity.

Would there be a genuine community without pain? Does not Stringfellow's insight that one is never alone in pain tell us something about our being-in-the-world, our being-in-relation? Is not being a "surrogate" of everyone else who hurts a way of being savior, of being here for others, of being understanding in the sense of experientially knowing and being able to put one's self in the place of the other?

It seems to me that the message of Jesus on the cross is the message of pain as intercessory and necessary for the humanization/divinization of the world.

24 SPELLBINDING JESUS

At the end of Matthew's seventh chapter comes the comment: "And the crowds were *spellbound* because Jesus spoke with authority, not as their scribes."

What is so interesting about this report is that it is perennially true. We find ourselves spellbound in the presence of a great teacher, a revealer of truth, and we find our hearts left cold in the presence of the professional "scribes" who say but do not do, who perform hollow acts, who sermonize about things that obviously mean little to them.

Jesus IS spellbinding. Every time we return to the gospels for a quiet moment, we hear him tell us something new. Perhaps it is because we change each day and, therefore, can hear the same words in a new way each time we go to them. Jesus does speak with authority. If the word authority means "one who gives and sustains and supports life," then surely Jesus speaks with this life-giving force because he speaks truth in a way that has sustained believers for 2000 years, even when his words have been heard differently by people who have been enculturated in a variety of ways. The authority of Jesus' words fills me with an awareness that he IS truth incarnate. He IS life.

He IS the way to wholeness (holiness). When I listen, I realize that his words are waiting for my listening. When I substitute something lesser, my ears should be affronted. When I read, I know that this message reveals depths of wisdom and perception that can be adapted by every generation and culture and can be seen as a guiding light to pierce the darkness of ignorance.

Jesus *is* a spellbinder. As Christians we cannot find meaning in life without him, and when we go looking for him in a serious way, we discover a new life, new meaning, new inner peace, new joy, new reason for living. Some may call this the experience of being "born again." Some may call it "putting on the new person." Some may call it resurrection. Whatever the name, the reality is known by its fruits, not by our attempts to define the mystery.

Spellbinder Jesus! Spellbind us all. Teach us to spend more time listening to you and then go forth with your new life in us to change this saddened world, sad because it does not listen to you and love the way you love.

25 BELIEVERS ARE BLESSINGS

During the past week, I looked into the steady open gaze of a believer. I knew that God was present and the moment when our eyes met was a personal blessing, an encounter with a real presence. It was the word made flesh once again.

That moment has been with me all week. I've reflected on the importance of such people in our lives. They remind us that we who get ourselves so caught up in "the new" sometimes act as though there is no "ahead." We materialize our lives without spiritualizing them. We act on a level that is less than human as a result of this dichotomy. It is truly human to live as enfleshed spirit or as spirited flesh.

True believers are indeed true blessings. I see those eyes yet, gazing into mine and asking that I, too, become a better believer. I know that this moment of grace is one of the ways revelation continues for those of us who live in the "now" testament age. Not the "old" testament time; not the "new" testament time, but the "now testament time." I know that revelation comes to us through one another and all of creation. I know that I, too, can be a blessing to others and the greater my belief in compassionate love, the greater blessing I can be to others.

Lord, help my unbelief. Make me a better blessing!

26 AM I A BIGOT?

So often we presume our own purity of intention in what we do, say, and believe. Yet, when I find myself judging the actions of other people, I rarely find myself judging their intention as "pure," unalloyed with a selfish, hidden agenda or a motivation based on ignorance or prejudice.

But when I simplify and put people into categories which I call "open" or "closed," I find that the people I put in the "closed" group are those who have very hard and narrow visions of reality and who can be mean and cruel in their relations to and judgments of others. These people often embrace the principles that reinforce their prejudices and protect them from taking the risk of walking outside the walls they have created to protect their own lives.

Because a lot of these people can be found on parish councils, in chancery offices, in educational establishments, in political leadership positions where their decisions affect the lives and happiness of so many others, I begin to worry about my own "building of walls" and my own narrow view of life. I see the awful injustice so often done by such bigots under the sugar coating of phrases that justify: "for the good of the church," "for the sake of democracy," "for the benefit of the company," etc.

It really alarms me to realize that my own "purity of intention" can be filled with the swill of bigotry, selfishness, and arrogance and that I can justify all this by pious phrases.

Ouch!

27 GETTING HOLY BY OURSELVES

There is an old heresy known as pelaganism that claims we can win heaven by our own efforts, we can become perfect by an act of our will. Every generation falls victim to this heresy in one form or another, and people who are blinded by this misguided belief eventually become frustrated, bitter, depressed, or give it all up entirely.

In our busy, over-productive, thing-centered culture we are so bombarded by the constant crappy commercials that we have no quiet time left to hear a voice that speaks from a dimension beyond our usual, mundane daily dreams.

Because we don't make enough quiet time for this kind of listening, we may never know the real tragedy of our deafness. It is quite often in these attentive, quietly listening times that we hear the word of God in a brand new and dazzlingly illuminating way — a way of hearing/seeing — a way of new knowing — a communication beyond words and sometimes beyond intuition.

I really believe that God is ever present in us but as smog blinds us to our everpresent sun, we are only dimly aware of this loving, life sustaining presence. We cannot by ourselves merit "deserving God by what we do," but we can do more to be open to "God's being with us."

Maybe this musing seems full of contradictions, but the paradox may be that we really have to "let go to let God."

One thing I do know: silent, centering time each day opens us to the reality of this dimension beyond the mundane one in which we live and move and have too much of our being.

28 That Rare Vessel of Election

*O*nce in a while one meets a person whose "chemistry" makes the person seem larger than his or her body. The space around is filled with that person's presence.

I may naively call this "aura." All I know is that when I come into such an orbit and feel this aura, I am in the presence of a very special person—a "vessel of election."

Last month I met such a "vessel of election" and the gift of that special presence remains with me still. I am a continent away, but I feel that I have been graced (gifted) by being with someone who understands me and lives as Christ's risen body in our space and time.

She is elected to be prophet and witness to a waiting world that needs healing and reconciling. She exudes this mission in the gentle intensity of open communication, childlike in trust, warm in acceptance, penetrating in conviction.

I was with her for three hours, but I truly know that the gift of that special time in her presence will be a blessing to me all my life. I can now be with her again through her writing. I can sit quietly with her *via* her books, and I can and do know that she is a living witness to the reality that she has been elected for the perpetual mission of salvation: saving people by loving and bringing out the best in them.

Meeting her made me want to spend the rest of my life becoming whole (holy) in the best sense of the word, and possibly becoming a vessel of election, too.

29 SILENCE AND MUTENESS

Wherever we go today, we seem to find constant noise that babbles incessantly about inconsequential things. Boxes are held to ears that listen to wild and raucous sounds that seem to deafen ears so they cannot listen to the sounds of silence. Yet, what is alarming is that sometimes, where there is silence, we find muteness.

So many people are unable to express who they are, what they want, what is meaningful to them, what their hopes are for the future. It is as though we are in that time in history when problems are so overwhelming that people sense the uselessness of expression. We see our TV programs turn to the frustration of violence and sadism. We see our art turn to psychotic incoherent privatized symbols that say little of value except to express chaos. We listen to lyrics that betray the emptiness of the lyric writer. We go to parties where people are afraid to say out loud what they really feel or fear or love or care about. We listen to counselors tell us that communication is necessary for humanity, but many of these confirm by their own lifestyles and failures that they, too, cannot communicate.

We seem to be into muteness that results from helplessness or a feeling of hopelessness, a feeling that there is "no use," "no future," "no sense. . . ." Is it just possible that this might be the very vacuum that is necessary before a new dawn can appear, a new birth, a new insight, a new life, a new way of knowing for the entire universe? Is it possible that we, as a culture that is over-saturated with things and non-necessities, with wants rather than needs met by built-in obsolesence creations, have had to come to a corporate *kenosis* so that we could be prepared to admit that we cannot save ourselves this way? Is this the time in history when we emit a global cry for salvation, when the mute voices speak, when the sounds of silence cease to be the barrenness of muteness, when we can once again listen to the good news?

Are we on the verge possibly, the edge possibly, of a new world where the lion and the lamb will lie down together and humankind will have another chance? Can we change the muteness in our silence into a cry for salvation, and when heard, respond to it with new life, new energy, new excitement, new reason for being?

Women understand the muteness of being unable to articulate. Our youth are now indicating that they understand. Can those who have not yet experienced muteness listen long enough and soon enough to know the meaning of these sounds of silence? Before it is too late for future life on mother earth?

30 THE LONELINESS OF DEPRESSION

In spite of all the books written about depression these days, one has to experience the reality before even beginning to understand the helpless loneliness of this all too pervasive malady.

Depression robs a person of life, vitality, energy. Even when a person's intellect knows what is happening, the body fails to respond to the act of the will. The command goes flabby.

Sometimes people who are depressed recognize depression in others but are so painfully preoccupied with survival themselves that they cannot reach out to assuage the other person's pain. Many times people who are depressed are misjudged and villified, ignored and hurt, and that only deepens the problem.

The causes of depression are as multiple as the pages of a dictionary, but the cure rests on the depressed person's ability to "hang in there" and struggle out of the dark cloud whenever a spot of sunlight shows. The struggle is a battle against giving up, the pinnacle between despair and hope.

Perhaps one of the symptoms is the inability to communicate, even the inability to speak at all. This only imprisons the person in darkness even further, so it is very important that there be a line of communication. If the voice goes mute and the mouth can't even open to speak, then a lifeline can be in dialogue with self or another through writing.

What is called journaling today may be similar to keeping a diary in the past. When old diaries are discovered and searched through, the reader can find revelations of secret pain, squashed dreams, lost hopes. A sensitive reader can also follow the writing and pick up key threads which, when woven together, reveal a continuing pattern running through the life recorded.

No doubt everyone gets depressed at times, but for some, these times are more like disappointments or balloon bursting. For others, these times are brief and can be coped with. For still others, each new depression deepens the furrow and makes each subsequent climbing out much more difficult. For some, this climbing out ultimately becomes impossible and they drop back into the dark chasm for the rest of their lives.

Perhaps one of the greatest acts of charity or ministry of love in this generation is to help depressed people cope and become well again. This takes time and patience, but it is a life-saving activity and, therefore, a divine action.

31 PARADOX

I recall hearing a news report a few years ago about Andrei Gromyko visiting Pope John Paul. The pope asked him if he were afraid of his army, the Swiss Guards. Gromyko was reported to have said that it is the least dangerous army in the world.

When I heard this, I rejoiced at the paradox and cried for the blindness of one who believed that military might meant strength. The real truth is that the pope's *unarmed* Swiss Guard represents the power which transcends all barriers and can't be shot down in Star Wars. The power of *armed* men is to destroy life, first others, and then themselves.

The contrast of two armies, one armed and one unarmed, is probably the current symbol of David and Goliath, but we never seem to learn the lesson. Today, our world totters under the burden of nuclear arms. The poor die hungry while we feed the military and the frustration and violence of all this evil spills over into what William Stringfellow calls "a prosperous period for death"—in short, "a dark age."

Perhaps because the age is so dark, we who call ourselves children of the light must ask what it means to be "the light of the world." Jesus tells us to let our light shine because humans need to see this light. Each of us must maintain our own spark, our own glimmer, our own light in spite of the crush of darkness, in spite of the fear the darkness brings, in spite of the terrific energy it takes to resist the forces of darkness and death.

One way to do this, I suspect, is to be true to that inner self which is God's real presence in a special way. The temptation to compromise, to give in, to give up, to give over to the enemy Goliath is so strong. Our little

David's slingshot or our little beam of light is more necessary than ever because each tiny pebble or each beam of light is a sign of hope for someone else who is going through the same struggle.

Well, Gromyko, the unarmed "army" may be the least dangerous after all, for they represent life and hope and future.

32 HEARING AND UNDERSTANDING

When Jesus said, "He who has ears to hear, let him hear," I suspect that because he spoke in parables, metaphors, and paradoxes, he was asking for the kind of hearing we call understanding. Understanding is *standing under the surface meaning* in order to get to the richer depths of what is being communicated.

So many books today are written about communication, yet it seems that for many people the closer they live to one another, the less they are able to communicate in an *understanding* way.

Spouses speak to one another but in all probability do not hear the hidden agenda. Spouses, team workers, etc., have a right to take literally what is being said in the sense that they have a right to the truth, a need to trust that the person speaking is being authentic. This, though, should only be the beginning. Then the heart has to listen and the heart knows how to listen in that deep way that the ear cannot hear.

What is so painful to many people who have to live close together is that the surface words reveal so much. Patterns emerge. Hidden fears and desires are betrayed or leaked out. When these revelations occur, it is imperative that it is the heart that listens and not the ear. Real love can absorb the ambiguities; fear cannot.

Perhaps Jesus's admonition, "He who has ears to hear, let him hear," should be taken as a great commandment. It would mean that he is asking us to "really listen" or to "hear with the heart," to understand. Under is a place of service, under is humble, under is meek, under is strength for supporting what is on top, under is mostly unknown, under is mainly unseen. Under is not noted. To be understanding is to know the Jesus who said, "I have come, not to be served but to serve."

He who has ears to hear, let him listen. She who has ears to hear, let her listen.

33 SUFFERING LEADS TO GLORY

Once one gets used to paradoxes, it isn't difficult to see that the stories Jesus told and the life he lived all point to opposites.

Glory is our expression for total joy and delight and fullness of everything. Suffering is our term for all that we try to avoid. Yet, what we try to avoid leads to what we hope for. Now there's the paradox!

When we get mail or a phone call from a family member or a friend who alerts us to the suffering of others, we grope for words to help them and find little success. What we do find is a deeper understanding of the importance of suffering for ultimate growth and fulfillment. Yet, we want to shield people from the pain, particularly the innocent who suffer as a result of the selfishness and thoughtlessness of others.

"It isn't fair!" is our first reaction. Someone nice gets an ulcer because someone else is not so nice. Yet, we are called on to forgive the "not-so-nice" who, in ignorance or arrogance, act so often the way we ourselves sometimes do toward others.

When the call comes to forgive someone for making someone else suffer needlessly, we have a bit of an insight into how God puts up with us and supports and loves us anyway. That's the marvel. That's the model. That's the challenge. And when we think about it a long time, and think about Jesus, his life, his suffering as a result of others, we get a glimpse of the marvelous truth that suffering leads to glory.

34 OUR NEED TO BE RIGHT

Every once in a while an excellent essay becomes a great gift of God. It is present to us at a time when we may need it most. At the very time when we think that time is measured chronologically, God intervenes with a surprise, with *kairos* time. I call this the grace or gift time. It is always like a Happy Birthday surprise.

One of these gifts for me was an essay in *Commonweal* (February 22, 1985) by John Garvey in which he made the profound observation:

> What we need is a truly radical humility, one which can abandon any need to be right. This is terribly difficult, because it could seem to be an indifference to truth. But our need to be right has nothing to do with any love of the truth at all.

What a revelation! And how true it is! Garvey's insight came at a time when *I* was *right* and that meant someone else was wrong. But if we understand what radical humility is, we might begin to understand what Jesus meant when he warned us not to confuse light and darkness in ourselves. And as I ponder about it, I have to admit that right and wrong are two sides of the same thing so often, and while I insist that the other look at my side, he or she is absorbed in the magnetism of the other side and wants me to see it that way.

Again the paradox, because five years from now I'll probably be campaigning for the other side unless I learn that radical humility means that I am called in this life to balance the dilemma and see both the "right and the wrong" on both sides. That breaks it up into quarters, and when I look again, the quarters can be broken down into eighths, and so on, until we come to the sparkling new awareness of the multiple facets of any created thing. Suddenly, then, with this new vision, we drop our narrow view and stand in awe and wonder at the mystery of interconnectedness and variety.

Perhaps this is where radical humility comes in. We begin to be aware of the real mystery of creation and we stand in ultimate awe. Is ultimate awe another name for radical humility?

35 HUMAN NATURE AND IDOLS

Saint Gregory of Nyssa is reported to have said that concepts create idols and only wonder comprehends anything. When I try to translate this into church life, I discover some frightening facts. I watch the idols we have created in our churches that we somehow find acceptable to worship without question, and I watch the wonder on the faces of people gathered at the Eucharist when a good homilist does what Jesus did: tell a story.

The story enfleshes the reality of people in their lives, their hopes, their accomplishments. The idol stands in cold splendor, and we bow to it uncomprehendingly. We have many idols in the rubrics which were once worship experiences of another age. Today, they are for us like Ezekiel's bones. We don't seem to be able to get new life into those dead bones any more than we can contradict Jesus's observation that you can't sew new cloth on an old garment without causing ultimate damage.

I suppose that if people were to list what they consider idols at worship and what they consider "wonder-events" at worship, we would have long lists on both sides. Wouldn't it be interesting to make such a list and then to analyze the outstanding qualities in the two columns?

Here are some of the idols I am expected to worship in public at this time in history but which I find deadening and bone-drying.

1. Styrofoam circles as a symbol of what Jesus asked us to do at the Last Supper.

2. Holding high the gospel book so that we may gaze up at it but so rarely have its riches explained and truly shared.

(The bread and the word are suppressed and kept from the very people who are told that they are coming to the "source and center" of our faith. We fail to understand the sharing of bread and life in his memory, and we fail to hear his words as broken open in story and our common language.)

The paradox here is that when people are not fed bread and word, they seek response to this need elsewhere. Some are successful; some are not. But the search ultimately creates new forms of life, new forms of worship, and ultimately new life. In this sense, idols ultimately indirectly cause new life and the dry bones begin to move in response to the "word of the Lord."

The idols in our churches and the idols in our government and the idols in our family and business lives so often result from so-called logical thinking—one side of the brain, one predominance suppressing the other. The awe and wonder and creative response to the world in surprise and delight mostly comes from the non-logical side of the brain. Is it possible that the day is on its way that we will come to wholeness by balancing these two sides, these two approaches to life? Can it be that salvation for the twenty-first century will be a church where inherited dogmas do not rule over lived experience, where so-called male logic does not rule over so-called female interconnected-caring way of seeing? Can it be that salvation for the world in this terrible dark age of death, violence, and suppression by the military will be experienced as we find a way to serve bread to all who come in need? As we speak the good news freely to all regardless of sex, color, or state in life? Where bread is bread for all? Where word is spoken freely, giving hope and life?

May the prophets who wonder and the poets who wonder lead us away from our idols and into their hope-filled joy.

36 FOREVER AMBER

Years ago the phrase "forever amber" conjured up the image of the title of a book. Today, when we find ourselves at a stop light that seems to be "forever amber," we find ourselves getting frustrated because we cannot go and we do not want to stay. We are caught in the "do-nothing" trap.

Yet, "forever amber" times have their own value. They are the buffer zones between safety and danger, between the green light indicating that all is well and the red light that warns of possible danger and a collision course.

American Catholic women have felt themselves to be in the forever amber zone long enough, and they are now opting for movement—either toward the safety signal of the *status quo* or the more dangerous "turning right on red" and into a zone where there will be a fight for the local turf.

Some women are content to conform to the pattern set out and unquestioned regardless of the inconvenience, the traffic jams, the questionable quality of direction, life style, ideology, and value suppositions. Other women have been listening to those who have long since moved out of the forever amber zone and have opted for growth, change, new risks, new life, and basically and most radically a new look at the gospels. It is these women who know that the more we understand and appreciate the radical call of the gospels, the more dangerous we are to the church.

This seeming paradox gets a nutshell comment from astute Rosemary Ruether who noted that American nuns who caught on to the call of the gospels as they moved into graduate and post graduate education in the 1960s and the 1970s are such a threat to the *status quo* hierarchy that the latter "is not pleased and is anxious to repress these people, even if it means destroying half the religious orders and driving half the nuns out" (*Sojourner's* interview, April, 1985). Ruether notes also that the "problem with the repression from the church is that you find the church hierarchy denying the gospel."

As shocking as this statement may sound to those who have not been listening, it is nothing new to the many women who have attempted to move beyond being forever amber where there is no decision making, no boat rocking, no determined choice unmotivated by fear or other pressure, such as a misunderstood or primitive religious response.

What seems to be evolving, though, is that women who join together in networking groups, base communities, scripture studies, or whatever, come to a new awareness of their own worth and power, and find that it really doesn't make sense to accept "traditions" unquestioningly, or support programs or projects that really do limit the potential for women's gifts to affect the world more completely and humanly.

What happens when people break out of a regular institutional form, whether a road system which may often impede transportation, or a church system which denies freedom to half of its people according to gender, or an economic system which refuses to face the consequences of injustice, is that a new form is born. In the newness is new energy and new hope and new life which contrasts to the old form.

As the new form is taking root, old forms dry up and crumble away. Sometimes this is an imperceptible process, and sometimes it happens quickly. Most of the time, there are many contributing factors that create the new possibility.

As the woman spirit rises, however, it will flow beyond the forever amber stage where it was controlled and it will confront the reds and the greens, and ultimately make a new color, a new form, a new life.

This is the process in today's church and it will not be forced back. Women are making the choice. They are no longer happy in the standing still state. (They never were!)

37 COMPASSION

In the pregnantly powerful and packed paragraphs of *Jesus in Focus,* author Gerard S. Sloyan includes many marvelous gems such as: "Compassion, quite simply, is the capacity to put yourself in someone else's shoes, since all are sufferers."

He then goes on to explain the difference between pity and compassion and points out how Jesus manifested the latter, over and over again.

Hearing the pain of sinners is the first step in acceptance and ultimately in "suffering with." I suspect that when we feel self-righteous, the emotion we have may be pity, but it can't be compassion. Thus, our becoming like Jesus means living like him in his acceptance and understanding of the suffering of others. He was never "above" or "apart" and therefore didn't "save from afar." As one New Testament writer put it, "He became one of us." That identification includes knowing suffering, and he did—all the suffering that stems from injustice, from control by foreign powers, from religious systems that put law above spirit, from physical deprivation (no place to lay his head, nothing to eat), from physical pain in its most exquisite ultimacy (crucifixion). It seems that for whatever reason we need to have compassion, Jesus has already been there experiencing pain, humiliation, deprivation, insults.

His patient acceptance of the so-called underside of life is our model as Christian and female in the space and time in which we find ourselves.

To suffer with—to go through the experience of living in someone else's shoes (as well as we can)—is probably the key to salvation for all. If all of us identified with the insecurities, fears, disappointments, and crushed hopes of others, we probably would find ourselves loving more and judging less.

It is helpful to be compassionate now for those in the clerical state who fear giving up their turf—the accretion of so-called power that has been misplaced over the centuries and erodes as adults study the history of their religious traditions.

To be in their shoes right now means to feel the rock turn to sand, to have our tunnel vision of life challenged (indeed by some of the documents of Vatican II still not accepted a quarter of a century later). The temptations are to choose life or to choose death—the former meaning that we must not stop the process of growth into new forms in each generation, and the latter meaning we choose to protect our power base by keeping people subservient to us and ignorant of their rights and our own lack of real power, which ultimately emanates from the Spirit.

With compassion, we can feel this tug of war. With compassion, we can encourage the move to "choose life."

Snorkeling is not something everyone does. When an opportunity to snorkel in the lucid waters of the Caribbean presents itself, however, one who usually doesn't, does!

It was when I came up from the new-to-me-world below the surface that I perceived a truth with great clarity. A man sitting on the shore was gazing across the turquoise and royal blue waters, watching a "luv boat" cruise ship gliding toward the dock. His perception of reality at that moment was all contained in the surface experience of watching the beautiful ship float to rest against the dock. He saw from the water up.

Because I had just seen both the above and below of the water's surface, I could "know" both worlds. Rather than likening it to double vision, I had, instead, a keen awareness of how we live our lives so often in one mode of knowing, unaware that there is both a height and depth we miss when we are limited to surface vision only. The underwater world revealed a multitude of creatures whose beauty was breathtaking. The coral, the plant life, the large number of brilliantly variegated fish announced an ecosystem which covers more of the surface of the globe than does the land and its inhabitants, my usual area of awareness. Yet, while fascinated with the beauty and largesse of underwater life, my mind had no time or interest for what might have been going on above.

The cruise ship would dock, disgorge its passengers, and the man sitting along the shore would be engaged in noting the heterogenity of human forms as they edged along the dock and melted into the waiting cabs to whisk them into the nearest town for that great activity of the consumer society—shopping for non-necessities and souvenirs usually destined to become ugly dust collectors at home.

I suppose that astronauts in outer space also have a vision different from the surface and the undersurface. All this makes me realize how difficult it is for us to believe that we all know, see, and comprehend the same things in the same way.

If I put the man on shore watching the cruise ship into a bishop's chair watching the people in his diocese, and the astronaut in the theologian's chair in a library carrel, and I the submerged woman who sees what others do not see into a politician's chair, where will that lead?

I suppose the chief message here is that we all live with some sort of tunnel vision; we can only focus on what is in our immediate environment most of the time. To have a global vision is difficult; to have it all together is to be divine-like. Perhaps the message from "above the sea" and "under the sea" is to remember that in seeing, we see so little. Aware of the little we see of the total will help us to hold back on judging the motives of others who also can only see from where they sit.

Those who sit in the same place all the time are doomed to see a small part of the whole. Those who move around and look at the world from a variety of viewpoints have a better chance of becoming whole themselves. Perhaps that is why putting trust in the views expressed by those who are institutionalized into one vision of reality is a dangerous thing. When I hear a bishop saying, "All Catholics believe such and such," I cringe inside because I know he is projecting *his* vision, not every Catholic's vision. When a congressman or a senator votes "my country right or wrong," I know he is projecting a view of reality from *his* precarious seat of temporary power. When I find myself deciding that it is time for women in the church to stand up and say a loud NO to male-created theologies that have no basis in human truth-experience, I must remember that all Catholic women do not have this vision—yet!

Yes, snorkeling is not something everyone does. But a marvelous moment of "double vision" when two worlds are seen at the same time is a great instigator to become more aware of how myopic we usually are.

39 DESOLATION

"Desolation is never God's voice."

That simple statement, uttered by a retreat master, was followed by the advice that we should never make a decision during desolation. Because desolation is so energy-consuming, it is so easy to drift into the darkness and see everything as black, useless, pain-filled, hellish.

If desolation is never God's voice, what could it be? It is the opposite of consolation, which breeds life, energy, hope, sunshine, love. If consolation sets us in the direction of what is good, true, and beautiful, desolation must influence us to go off course and into the wrong direction for fullness of life. Desolation, then, can be an obstacle, a temptation, a delusion. Whatever we call desolation, it has that swampy power to suck us into its dark hole, and fighting it takes all the mental and emotional muscle power we have sometimes. Perhaps the struggle is the process and the important thing. Perhaps the struggle against desolation is the activity by which we come to see that life is so often a struggle between the poles of light and darkness.

How many women, in the dark depths of desolation, have given up the struggle to work for a more gospel-oriented parish, for an adult education program that helps Catholics probe the real questions of adulthood in a community of believers searching for the best answers in ambiguous situations? How many of us recognize desolation in others and offer a helping support system until these people can pull out and stand on their own again? I see and hear from many women in church circles for whom the word desolation is not too strong. This is where we need the "saving community" most—people handlocked and heartlocked together to pull others out of the swamp and into new life. Perhaps this is another term for salvation. If desolation is never God's voice, I have a feeling that consolation is always God's voice—and gift.

40 Behold the Man!

Sometimes only a phrase or two from the Bible acts as a beam of light, giving us a much larger vision.

Pontius Pilate's phrase, "Behold the man," is such a beam. He exclaimed it as Jesus appeared before the crowd wearing a crown of thorns and a purple robe, attire given Jesus in derision, but satire has its own truth. The man in royal color and in crown was king, indeed, but of a kingdom of loving hearts, not the kingdom of imperial Rome or any other kingdom where justice, truth, and the value of life have had no role.

What I can't help thinking about is another "upside down" view. The signs of royalty—crowns and purple—carry their own burdens.

The man, *the* man for others, is always clad in purple and always wears a crown of thorns. Anyone who becomes "a man" in the fullest sense of the word "be ye fully integrated [perfect?] as your heavenly Father," must live with the two sides of the coin. We pay the price of integration and wholeness and being fully human by accepting the reality that we are both pleasure and pain, joy and sorrow, free and slave.

Behold the man—unjustly accused yet innocent, scourged for no crime except being an object of jealousy, royally in command of himself while being ridiculed by soldiers who took unlawful commands from others. Behold the man—dressed in symbols of royalty—regal purple and a painful crown.

Don't we all wear painful crowns when our heads spin with decisions which tear us apart? Doesn't anyone in any leadership role whatsoever feel the thorns of having to decide for one and against another? Doesn't maturity demand living with thorns from which there is no escape except the "escape" of Jesus: genuine and grateful acceptance of the human condition?

And don't we all wear the royal purple as we do our "kingly" tasks in life: creating order out of disorder when possible to give and sustain life and make things new, being source of energy and hope and leadership for others?

Yes, the more I ponder "Behold the man," I hear the definition of what it means to be hu-man or wo-man, the throne and the purple come together, but the integration of the symbol of pain and the symbol of glory can only be fulfilled in the one man Jesus and in us as we become one in him.

41 GOD THE SQUANDERER

Ruth Burrows, an English contemplative nun, calls God a self-squanderer who "is always giving himself insofar as he *can* be received, and he is always trying to enlarge the capacity so that he can give himself more fully."

This insight makes us realize that, like the sun, God is always there shining love on us, but we so often move out of the sunlight into the darkness of our own making. We freely choose not to be in a position to accept the gifts of light, warmth, life, love.

At the same time, God freely chooses to be permanently present to us and for us. The "self-squanderer" is ever-present to all of us as pure gift, and we are free to accept in gratitude and joy or refuse in fear because this love will eventually transform us.

We keep holding on to ourselves because we are afraid of the very love that casts out fear. We protect our smallness by naming those who open to this love a bit "kooky" or strange. Yet underneath this shell of ridicule, we secretly admire our heroes and our saints and admit we need them to urge us on to openness and trust and total gratitude as well. Responding totally to the "self-squanderer" is what makes us free, happy, secure, and whole.

Every time I forget that the truth I see out of my Western culture eyes is Western culture truth, I like to be reminded that the people who have lived in the East have a lot of truth to share with us. Listening to the East fills me with hope many times.

Buddhism, for example, expresses "reality's underside as well as its grandeur." We in the West want to separate good and evil and pretend that they do exist separately. The insight of the East recognizes that state in which one power operates in "curses and blessings," in sin and virtue, in good and evil, in weakness and strength, in hope and despair, all the time. We are both/and, not either/or most of the time.

This insight helps me to accept the fact that reality *is* two sides of the one thing *at once* and *all the time.* We cannot pretend that the other side does not exist. If we do, we live in a world of half-truth.

I remember an astute priest trained in catechetics telling a group of religion teachers that we do not face reality in our Christian Sunday schools and religious education because we only focus on one half of the human psyche. We talk about love, virtue, and goodness but fail to help our children understand that life will consist of knowing how to face evil and its intricate ramifications in their lives.

I try to recall that gem of wisdom every time I forget that I cannot "make someone else over to my image and likeness." I do not always manage to recall it, but when I do, I am more lenient, and I understand that when Jesus told the parable about the wheat and the weeds growing together—and how they should be allowed to grow together—he was giving us the wisdom of the East—reality IS good/bad, black/white, upstairs/downstairs, hate/love all at once, all the time.

---

43 A WOMAN AT THE WELL

One of the many surprises we can learn about ourselves comes when we go back into our past and note how much we have changed, particularly in our understanding of the meaning and value of life.

I came across a little piece of blank verse I wrote twenty years ago. The more I pondered over it, the more I discovered that the change in me occurred as a result of my new understanding of the biblical story. During the past twenty years, I had read so many scholarly interpretations of the story. This deepened my insight into life's meaning, for others and for myself.

Yet, I also discovered that what I had written twenty years ago contained a core of truth that will remain, for me, a lifelong call, a lifelong task—to move into new life willingly, to strive to be a Jesus-presence for others.

And so, I, too, stand—a woman at the well of life—invited to face myself and my "five men" (false idols? betrayals? substitutions for Christian living? shallow diversions from firmer commitments?).

Here is how I understood it twenty years ago:

The Woman at the Well

The way to freedom's long
and lonely, each decision
to take the next hard step
demanding much more giving
than what we've done before.

Sometimes, for less, we settle
and compromise each day—
the stagnant water will suffice—
the clear reveals too much!

There's a woman in John's gospel
who resembles this sad truth:
her waterpot's the symbol
of life that's not fulfilled
but filled with unfulfillments
like *five* men—not just one.

The Way, the Truth, the Life
now comes upon her scene
and speaks of *running water*
—of *life* she's yet to know.
So she *leaves her water jar.*
The living water He would give
has no need of water pots,
but bubbles high in human hearts
and *new life* blooms and grows.
She is transformed. Her mind is set.
She has a change of heart
and hurries off to *share* good news—
too good to keep for self.

This pouring out, this overspill
is the lesson we must catch.
Like her,
we must have love enough
to turn away
from our own kind
of deep stagnation,
to live a life
that *is* new life
fresh and fulfilling
for it is His—
His life in us.

I went back to the Bible and John's Chapter Four to take another look twenty years later and discovered a flood of new images, thoughts, and truths. This time, it wasn't the Samaritan woman who stood at the well. It was this middle-class North American woman standing there.

But Jesus had not changed. He was still the weary, dusty, fatigued traveller asking, "Give me a drink." He was still the poor pilgrim hunted and haunted in his own country, seeking safety and sanctuary in Samaria. And he was still the understanding, compassionate sojourner who offered the woman more in return. ("Quench my thirst now and I will quench yours in a far more wonderful and satisfying way.")

Somehow this is where divine and human meet, where helpless and helping, weakness and strength, instant and eternal, come together in liberating unity.

Somehow, once again, we are all at the well and Jesus is coming by once again, in human weakness, and he is asking us to pay attention so that we can understand the gift of life and the meaning of salvation in a new way.